# HATSHEPSUT

First published in North America in 2005 by
The National Geographic Society
1145 17th Street N.W.
Washington, D.C. 20036-4688

Copyright © 2005 Marshall Editions
A Marshall Edition
Conceived, edited, and designed by Marshall Editions
The Old Brewery, 6 Blundell Street, London N7 9BH, U.K.
www.quarto.com

Trade ISBN: 0-7922-3645-9
Library ISBN: 0-7922-3646-7
Library of Congress Cataloging-in-Publication Data available on request.

Originated in Hong Kong by Modern Age
Printed and bound in China by Midas Printing Limited

Design: Two Associates
Series editor: Miranda Smith
Picture research: Caroline Wood

For Marshall Editions:
Publisher: Richard Green
Commissioning editor: Claudia Martin
Senior Art Editor: Ivo Marloh
Picture manager: Veneta Bullen
Production: Anna Pauletti

For the National Geographic Society:
Art director: Bea Jackson
Project editor: Virginia Ann Koeth

Consultant: Dr. Joyce Tyldesley is Honorary Research Fellow in Egyptian Archaeology at the University of Liverpool, England.

Previous page: Hatshepsut, represented as a sphinx, wears the false beard that was part of the dress of the kings of ancient Egypt.
Opposite: An Egyptian sailing boat journeys down the River Nile.

# HATSHEPSUT

## THE PRINCESS WHO BECAME KING

### ELLEN GALFORD

WASHINGTON, D.C.

# CONTENTS

## BIRTH OF A PRINCESS

**1**

## A PALACE CHILDHOOD

**2**

# QUEEN
# AND MOTHER

**3**

# PHARAOH OF EGYPT

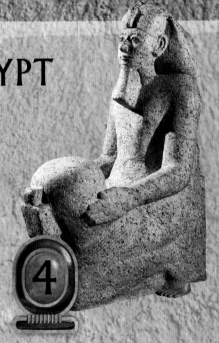

**4**

# BIRTH OF A PRINCESS

# Baby Hatshepsut

In a palace garden near the River Nile, Queen Ahmose, wife of Pharaoh Tuthmosis I of Egypt, had just given birth to a girl. Egyptians believed that a person could only be truly alive if they had a name, and it was a mother's task to choose it, at the very moment of birth. The queen had to say aloud the name of her daughter: "Hatshepsut."

The name meant "the foremost of women." And it turned out to be true in a way that no one, not even the baby's mother, could ever have expected. Hatshepsut would achieve the apparently impossible.

**Left: This 18th-dynasty earthenware jar is in the shape of the lion-headed god Bes, protector of women in childbirth.**

**Previous page: In this Egyptian limestone painting, a woman nurses her child while receiving tributes for its birth.**

Due to the problem of precisely dating Egyptian events, all the dates given are approximate. "c." is an abbreviation of "circa," meaning "about."

c. 3500 B.C.
The first sailing boats are in use on the River Nile.

She would not only become the "foremost of women," but the foremost of all people in the kingdom. She would do something that few of her sex had done, or would do again, in over 4,000 years of Egyptian history. For 22 years in the 15th century B.C., she would rule Egypt not as a queen but as its king—a female pharaoh.

On the day Hatshepsut came into the world, no one would have dared to think about her future. For mother and baby alike, this was a dangerous time. Women often died in childbirth, and many newborns did not survive long. Although Egyptian doctors took pride in their medical knowledge, their treatments were often based on magic rather than science.

To protect themselves and their unborn babies, mothers-to-be carried amulets—small objects that were believed to have magical powers. One type of amulet thought to be particularly effective was a curved ivory wand decorated with images of the gods and spirits who looked after pregnant women. On these amulets there were carved spells and good wishes, such as "Protection by night and day!"

## Hair magic

Egyptian women in labor wore tight ponytails and untied them just before the baby came. They believed that loosening their hair would magically ensure an easy birth.

## Mothers-to-be

Just as women do today, Egyptian mothers-to-be massaged themselves with perfumed oils to keep their skin soft and free of the stretch marks of pregnancy.

c. 3000 B.C.
Wild asses are tamed for domestic use in the Nile Valley.

c. 2925 B.C.
The two separate lands of Egypt are unified under King Menes.

All babies were born at home. Every family tried to create a special quiet space for a birth to take place. Poor families, living in mud-brick houses, might only be able to screen off a corner of a room. But royal ladies and the wives of rich men enjoyed the luxury of specially built birthing pavilions. Because the Egyptian climate was warm and sunny all year round, these pavilions were often set up outdoors, in courtyards, gardens, or on the flat roofs of houses. They were made of columns of papyrus stalks, decorated with vines and tendrils. The columns supported walls made of plants, and roofs made of woven matting.

When the moment came, the delivery of a child was strictly women's business. Male doctors did not attend a birth, and even the father was expected to keep away. Instead, a woman relied on close female relatives and trusted friends to act as midwives. They would hold her tightly and comfort her as she squatted on the ground, or perched on smooth bricks that had been given a special blessing.

After she was named, Hatshepsut was washed and given to her mother to hold.

Above: Containers in the shape of a nursing mother, such as this painted clay example dating from the New Kingdom, were used to store human milk—a popular remedy for childhood diseases.

c. 2900 B.C.
Paper is first made in Egypt by layering the papyrus reed.

c. 2900–2150 B.C.
The Pyramids and the Great Sphinx are built.

But, because she was a queen, Ahmose would not do the day-to-day work of feeding and caring for her daughter. Instead, she had chosen Sitre, one of the ladies of her court, as royal nurse. It was a great honor for any woman to be given this work. Sitre and her family later became important people in the land of Egypt.

When the queen had held her daughter, she handed Hatshepsut to Sitre, and the nurse placed the little princess on a cushion and carried her into the palace. According to custom, Queen Ahmose would have to stay in the pavilion for 14 days. When that time was over, she would return to palace life and hold a feast to celebrate her baby's birth.

**Below: This copy of a damaged 19th-dynasty papyrus shows a woman giving birth, attended by a midwife and her helpers. The two figures on the right wear the headdresses of a god and goddess.**

**c. 2800 B.C.**
Mummification of the dead is first practiced in Egypt.

**c. 2000 B.C.**
A city starts to grow at Thebes.

# A 4,000-Year History

4000 B.C     3500 B.C.     3000 B.C.     2500 B.C.     2000 B.C.

### PREDYNASTIC PERIOD
### c.3300–2925 B.C.

During this period Egypt existed as two separate lands—Upper Egypt, in the south, along the upper reaches of the River Nile, and the more northerly land of Lower Egypt, closer to the Mediterranean Sea, in the fertile Nile Delta.

### EARLY DYNASTIC PERIOD
### c.2925–2658 B.C.

According to legend, the two Egypts were first united under a king named Menes. His successors—the rulers of the 1st, 2nd, and 3rd dynasties—forged the foundations of an Egyptian state.

### OLD KINGDOM
### c.2658–2150 B.C.

Egypt grew rich and confident under the 4th-dynasty kings. The Sphinx and the Pyramids of Giza were built, and the art of writing with hieroglyphs was well established. The empire expanded southwards, conquering Nubia.

### SECOND INTERMEDIATE PERIOD
### c.1750–1550 B.C.

Weakened once again by internal splits, Egypt found itself an easy target for conquest by a people known as the Hyksos. Hyksos kings identified themselves as pharaohs, but Theban warrior-kings rose up and drove them out.

### NEW KINGDOM
### c.1550–1076 B.C.

The pharaohs of the 18th dynasty restored Egyptian glory, building an empire that was stronger than ever. Conquest and trade made them wealthy and increasingly sophisticated, leading to new directions in the arts and—briefly— to a new religion.

### THIRD INTERMEDIATE PERIOD
### c.1076–712 B.C.

This period brought a split once again. The south of Egypt was the subject of a military coup; the north fell to local nobles. Foreign neighbors—Libyans from the west, followed by Nubians to the south— moved in and took control.

### FIRST INTERMEDIATE PERIOD
**c.2150–2100 B.C.**

Egypt broke into two kingdoms again. In the south, a group of Theban noblemen established a new dynasty, declaring themselves the true heirs to the old pharaohs. But their northern neighbors ignored these claims.

### MIDDLE KINGDOM
**c.2100–1750 B.C.**

Egypt was reunited by the strong governments of the pharaohs of the 11th and 12th dynasties. These kings brought about a rebirth of arts and culture, revived foreign trade, and sponsored irrigation projects, which increased food production.

### LATE PERIOD
**c.712–332 B.C.**

Foreign conquerors came in waves. Assyrians and Persians absorbed Egypt into their own great Asian empires. The 31st dynasty gave way to the unstoppable Greek forces of Alexander the Great. Egypt's line of independent rulers had come to an end.

### GRECO-ROMAN PERIOD
**c.332 B.C.–A.D.395**

Egyptians would no longer be masters of their own land. Alexander the Great's later successor— the celebrated queen Cleopatra—was defeated by Rome in 30 B.C., and Egypt stayed under Roman control until that empire fell.

## HATSHEPSUT

Hatshepsut belonged to the 18th dynasty of pharaohs. This line of Theban kings ruled Egypt at the start of the period known as the New Kingdom, and took the country into a new golden age. Hatshepsut's exact date of birth is unknown, but she ruled Egypt for 22 years and died, probably aged somewhere between 35 and 55 years, in spring, 1482 B.C.

# A Royal Family

Hatshepsut's father, Pharaoh Tuthmosis I, had no royal blood in his veins. He was a mighty general who had won great victories against Egypt's foreign foes. The pharaoh he served, Amenhotep I, had no sons to inherit the throne. Amenhotep believed that Tuthmosis had the wisdom and the courage to rule the kingdom well. So he chose him as his successor.

> *"His Majesty… found that the enemy was gathering troops. Then his Majesty made a great heap of corpses among them."*
> **From the tomb of Ahmose, a military man, c. 1500 B.C.**

Although there was no family connection between the old pharaoh and the new, both men were heirs to a proud tradition. They were strong and talented warrior-kings who came from Thebes, in southern Egypt. It was thanks to these Thebans that Egypt—after two centuries of chaos and conquest by foreign rulers—once more found itself united as a single kingdom. Safe again in their hands, Egypt was becoming rich and powerful.

When he became pharaoh, Tuthmosis opened the royal treasuries. With these riches, he sent his armies southwards into Nubia and northeastwards across the Sinai into Asia. From the River Euphrates on the edge of present-day Iraq and south into the African lands beyond the third cataract of the River Nile, they spilled the blood of many neighbors and built an empire.

**c. 2000 B.C.**
The building of a temple at Karnak in Egypt begins.

**c. 1550 B.C.**
The New Kingdom and the 18th dynasty begin under Pharaoh Ahmose I.

Returning home in triumph from these campaigns, Tuthmosis began to plan for the kingdom's future. The pharaoh of Egypt could have as many wives as he wished, but only one could hold the rank of queen. As far as is known, Queen Ahmose bore only daughters—Hatshepsut herself, and a little princess called Neferubity who died when she was still a baby. But Hatshepsut had several half-brothers. Her father would name one of these princes to succeed him on Egypt's throne.

**Left: Sculpted in pink granite, Hatshepsut is here shown wearing a king's headdress, looking calm and stately.**

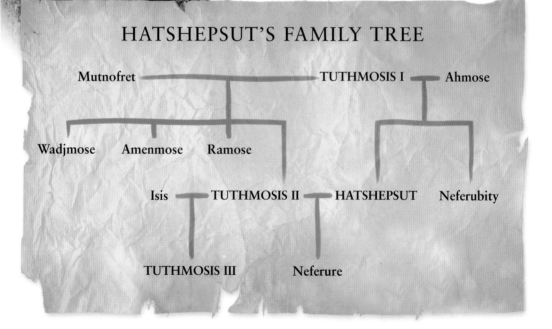

## HATSHEPSUT'S FAMILY TREE

Mutnofret ———————— TUTHMOSIS I —— Ahmose

Wadjmose    Amenmose    Ramose

Isis —— TUTHMOSIS II —— HATSHEPSUT    Neferubity

TUTHMOSIS III    Neferure

**c. 1550 B.C.**
Irrigation by shadoof, a bucket on a swivelling pole, is introduced in Egypt.

# Gods and Goddesses

From an early age Hatshepsut would have known that she belonged to the most important family in the land. But she would soon have realized that another family, far greater than her own, ruled the lives of everyone in the kingdom. Its members were the all-powerful and terrifying gods and goddesses of Egypt.

Egyptians worshiped many gods. Some were local deities, connected to a particular place and known only to the people who lived there. Others had—over the thousands of years of Egyptian history—become known and worshiped throughout the land. Certain gods were called different names in different places. Often gods changed their identities over time, or two gods merged into one. Hatshepsut would have learned the gods' names and heard stories about them from her nurse or at her mother's knee.

**Left: Amen-Min-Kamutef—a mixture of the god Amen and the fertility-god Min—appears in a painting from Tuthmosis III's temple at Deir el-Bahri.**

c. **1535** B.C.
Tuthmosis I, father of Hatshepsut, becomes pharaoh of Egypt.

c. **1532** B.C.
Hatshepsut's half-brother, Tuthmosis, is born.

She knew that these all-powerful beings lived in great stone temples built for them by her father and by the pharaohs before him. Every year, her home city of Thebes was the scene of great religious festivals, when the statues of the gods were carried through the streets in processions, and ferried on

Right: The queenly mother-goddess Hathor took several different forms. She appeared as a beautiful woman with a pair of horns on her head, and as a cow.

magnificent barges up and down the Nile.

Hatshepsut would have known exactly what these wonderful beings looked like. Unlike humans, they could take on the shapes and forms of animals. The god Horus, for instance, who gave kings the power to rule, had the sharp eyes and curved beak of a falcon.

Everyone felt close to the gods. They loved them, feared them, and asked them for help and favors in their prayers. But for Hatshepsut and her family, the connection was even stronger. Egyptians believed that their pharaoh acted as a living bridge between the world of mortals and the gods themselves.

## Hatshepsut's gods

**AMEN** King of all the gods
**BES** Protector of women in childbirth
**HATHOR** Goddess of music, love, and human fate
**HORUS** Sky-god and protector of kings
**ISIS** Mother-goddess and inventor of agriculture
**OSIRIS** God of the underworld and of vegetation
**RE** The sun-god
**SEKHMET** Goddess of war and disease
**THOTH** God of wisdom

c. **1530** B.C.
Hatshepsut is born.

# A PALACE
# CHILDHOOD

# The Life of a Princess

For the young Hatshepsut, home was a palace. The royal toddler spent her time in airy rooms decorated with bright tiles, soft rugs, and carved wooden pillars. Outdoors, under the watchful eye of her nurse Sitre, she played in sheltered gardens, dabbling her fingers in ponds full of darting fish.

Although Hatshepsut had a troop of servants to care for her, her mother was never far away. There would be frequent visits to the queen's chamber, where Ahmose, like other 18th-dynasty queens before her, rested on a couch which had legs shaped like a lion's paws.

Hatshepsut would have seen much less of her father. Thebes was his official capital city, but Tuthmosis spent most of his time traveling through the kingdom with his court officials and scribes, moving up and down the River Nile on the royal barge.

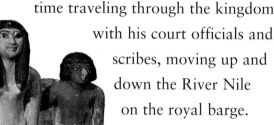

Left: The figures of this Egyptian man and his family are painted in color code—males have red skin, females yellow.

Previous page: The 18th-dynasty Princess Meketaten wears the mark of childhood—a braided sidelock dangles from her head.

c. 1528 B.C.
Neferubity, Hatshepsut's baby sister, is born.

Right: This wooden cat has bronze teeth and a jaw that can open and close. It was carved by a New Kingdom Theban craftsman, probably as a child's toy.

He spent only a few nights at a time in one of his several riverside palaces. These palaces were known as the "Mooring Places of the Pharaoh." The rest of the royal family rarely—if ever—joined him on his journeys. The queen had her own private residence, while the pharaoh's other wives and their children lived together in a large palace of their own.

Busy as he was, however, Tuthmosis would have taken a great interest in the welfare and education of his children. And, even when her parents were busy with their royal duties, Hatshepsut would rarely have been alone. She would have spent time with her father's other children, and with children whose parents were members of the court. The pharaoh often invited important Egyptian nobles to send their youngsters to live and study alongside the royal children. This was considered a great honor, and those who received it would proudly call themselves "children of the palace" forever after.

## Egyptian toilets

The toilet in an Egyptian palace was a low, wooden stool with a large hole cut in the seat. A shallow box full of sand, like a cat's litter tray, stood underneath.

c. **1528–1524** B.C.
Neferubity dies.

The children of Hatshepsut's nurse Sitre would also have been likely playmates. There was a special lifelong bond between the offspring of a royal nurse and the prince or princess she fed and cared for.

Hatshepsut would have had a nursery overflowing with toys and games. Courtiers and servants presented her with wonderful gifts, created specially for her by the finest craftsmen in the land. She would have owned any number of brightly striped balls, rattles, and spinning-tops. Her wooden pull toys would have been in the shapes of cats and crocodiles. Complete with gleaming glass eyes, these would have had bronze teeth set into jaws that could snap open and shut.

Even the poorest Egyptian children owned simple dolls made of rags and carved wood. Hatshepsut would have had dolls of painted wood or ivory, dolls with moving arms and legs, tiny carved mothers with even tinier babies perched on their backs, dolls that danced, dolls with different changes of clothing, and enough wonderfully carved pieces of doll-sized furniture to fill a miniature palace.

## Palace job titles

Palace servants included the Superintendent of the Storerooms, Superintendent of the Kitchens, Superintendent of the Bakehouse, Preparers of Sweets, Bearers of Cool Drinks, Scribe of the Sideboard (Butler), maids, porters, gardeners, and underservants.

Above: Throughout Egypt's history, craftsmen carved small figures, probably for play. This painted wooden doll dates from c. 500 B.C.

c. 1525–1518 B.C.
Tuthmosis I captures exotic animals to add to his private zoo.

c. 1520 B.C.
Tuthmosis I celebrates his Sed festival, marking 15 years of his reign.

If they grew bored with all these toys, Hatshepsut and her friends could play board games and games of skill, and do dances with complicated steps. Like most Egyptian homes, the palace had its pets—birds, kittens, puppies, and even monkeys with their own jeweled bracelets and necklaces.

Hatshepsut's father owned some pets of a very different kind. On special occasions, the royal children might have been taken on a visit to the pharaoh's menagerie—his private zoo—to see the lions, leopards, cheetahs, ostriches, elephants, giraffes, and other exotic creatures. Many of these were sent to Egypt as gifts from foreign kings. Others were collected by the pharaoh himself. Even in wartime, the pharaoh and his generals amused themselves between battles by hunting animals to kill or capture.

**Above: The animals on this 12th-century B.C. papyrus are probably playing senet, a popular game that was like chess or checkers.**

**c. 1520 B.C.**
Tomb-building is under way at the Valley of the Kings.

# Dress at Court

Living in a hot and sunny country, Egyptians did not force their babies and small children into clothes. As a child, Hatshepsut almost certainly wore something like a modern diaper, probably made of strips of linen cloth. But after she outgrew the need for that kind of protection, she would have happily scampered about the palace wearing nothing at all.

Above: Sennefer, Mayor of Thebes, and his wife Meryt are shown wearing the typical clothes of noblemen and -women on a wall in his 18th-dynasty tomb.

However, when there was a time or a reason for getting dressed up, Hatshepsut would have had a large supply of beautiful garments that she could wear, including carefully stitched shawls and robes, and delicately pleated linen dresses. Because she was a princess, and like the other members of the royal household, her clothes would be made with rich materials, and the needlework used to make them would have been of the highest quality.

c. 1520–1518 B.C.
Tuthmosis I renovates the Temple of Amen at Karnak.

As she grew older, Hatshepsut would have adopted the sophisticated style of New Kingdom court ladies, wearing long, clinging dresses, and elaborately fringed and pleated robes. Men of the time dressed in kilts and skirts, with fringed sashes and pleated aprons, and a wide-sleeved tunic.

**Mirror mirror**

For mirrors, Egyptians used shiny discs of bronze or other metals, polished hard enough to give a good reflection.

Wealthy Egyptian women spent a lot of time on their makeup. Queen Ahmose, like every other lady at court, had her own prized collection of beautifully shaped pots and tubes to hold cosmetics. She would use a tiny brush to paint heavy, black lines around her eyes, and a powdered cloth gave her cheeks a rosy blush. Helped by her maid, she would cover her head with a stiffly styled wig made of human hair. Hatshepsut's father, like all upper-class men of the period, wore an elaborate wig, too.

Jewelry was popular with both sexes. Large, dangly earrings were a new fashion that was gradually becoming popular with courtiers. Other ornaments included rings, armbands, bracelets, anklets, broad collars made from row upon row of colored beads, headbands adorned with fresh flowers, and metal diadems studded with semi-precious stones.

Above: This jeweled diadem was brought to Hatshepsut's successor, Tuthmosis III, by one of three Syrian ladies joining his harem.

c. 1520–1503 B.C.
Hatshepsut's half-brothers Wadjmose, Amenmose, and Ramose die.

# Digging Up the Past

Around 1497 B.C., Hatshepsut ordered her architect and advisor, Senenmut, to construct her a mortuary temple at Deir el-Bahri near Thebes. The temple was called Djeser-Djeseru ("Holiest of the Holy") and featured carvings showing Hatshepsut's divine birth as well as her ships' expedition to the land of Punt. After Pharaoh Hatshepsut's death, someone, perhaps her step-son and successor Tuthmosis III, had her images chiselled off the walls of the temple. It was more than 3,000 years later that archaeologists first turned their attention to the site—and slowly uncovered the story of Hatshepsut.

Left: A team of laborers, photographed in 1894, pause during the excavations of Hatshepsut's temple at Deir el-Bahri. The archaeological work began on the site in 1881 and has continued right up to the present day.

Left: A photograph, taken after excavations were under way, shows the massive scale of the Deir el-Bahri temples. They were cut out of the rock by ancient Egyptian workers, but only unearthed by archaeologists centuries later.

In 1871, the tomb-robbing el-Rassul family discovered royal mummies in the cliffs at Deir el-Bahri. The French Egyptologist Gaston Maspero (left) oversaw the mummies' unwrapping. They had been moved out of their original tombs by order of a pharaoh from a later dynasty. One of them was Hatshepsut's successor, Tuthmosis III.

Above: In 1893, the Swiss archaeologist Henri Edouard Naville began 13 years of careful excavation at Deir el-Bahri. Other archaeologists doubted his theories, but without his efforts the extraordinary life and reign of Hatshepsut might have remained forever lost. In this 1894 photo he stands before a stone doorway. It was his work on the site that uncovered the buried glories of Hatshepsut's monument.

# Egyptian Education

The official nurses and others who cared for all the royal children came from the nobility. As well as her beloved Sitre, Hatshepsut would have had one or more male guardians. These courtiers, known as "father-tutors" or "father-nurses," would have supervised her upbringing.

Left: Egyptians wrote in pictures, or hieroglyphs, like these from Hatshepsut's temple at Deir el-Bahri.

The royal family had its own school, where carefully selected tutors taught the palace children reading, writing, arithmetic—and probably singing. Although there is no proof that Hatshepsut joined her male siblings in these sessions, archaeological evidence suggests that some Egyptian women knew how to read and write. As the pharaoh's daughter, Hatshepsut probably received a good education.

There are many references in Egyptian literature to the education of children. In Thebes, boys studied in temples, with priests as their teachers. Classes may have taken place outdoors, as it was usually warm and dry.

Boys began school at the age of five or six. They learned to read by reciting the words from ancient books out loud. They chanted the old-fashioned language until they had it memorized.

c. 1518 B.C.
Hatshepsut marries Tuthmosis, her half-brother.

## EGYPTIAN HIEROGLYPHS

| | | | | | | |
|---|---|---|---|---|---|---|
| a | f | kh | t | i | m | z |
| t | y | n | s | d | a | r |
| sh | d | w | h | q | plural | b |
| h | k | sw | p | ch | g | pr |
| abstract | movement | mammal | sun, time | a man | people | vegetation |

To practice writing, they copied wise sayings, business letters, and poems from texts put together specially for that purpose.

To persuade their pupils to concentrate, teachers used physical violence. One of their favorite sayings was: "A boy's ear is on his back. You have to beat him to make him listen." Children were also given plenty of homework. A collection of ancient Egyptian writings quotes a father's reminder to his son: "You have to bring your exercises daily. Be not idle!"

Boys learned to read, write, and work with numbers. Some of them later, as government officials, priests, and senior army officers, ran the country. The pharaoh's Egypt could not have survived without them.

c. 1518 B.C.

Tuthmosis I dies and his son,
Tuthmosis II, becomes pharaoh.

# Feasts and Festivals

Egyptians loved to celebrate and entertain. At court, Hatshepsut would have attended dinner parties with other members of the royal family and their guests. She would also have taken part in religious festivals and state occasions, such as the anniversary of her father's accession to the throne.

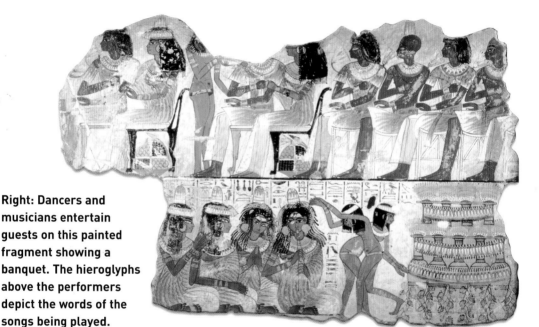

**Right: Dancers and musicians entertain guests on this painted fragment showing a banquet. The hieroglyphs above the performers depict the words of the songs being played.**

Palace banquets were a feast for all the senses. Guests sat on cushioned chairs at tables decorated with garlands of lotus blossoms and other flowers. As they chatted, they offered each other the most fragrant buds and blossoms. Singers, musicians, dancers, and acrobats entertained the guests.

**c. 1517 B.C.**
Tuthmosis II sends troops to Nubia to crush a rebellion.

Male and female servants carried in platters of home-grown and foreign foods: roast goose, beef from cattle fed on a special diet to make the meat moist and tender, fish from the palace's own well-stocked ponds, fresh vegetables and herbs, figs and pomegranates from Queen Ahmose's garden, dozens of different breads and cakes, sweetmeats flavored with date syrups and honey. Wines and beers of the finest quality flowed from glass vessels and ceramic jars.

Only the royal family and the wealthiest nobles enjoyed such feasts. However, all the pharaoh's subjects, rich and poor, could share in the excitement of public festivals. Every year, Hatshepsut and her brothers could have looked down from their balconies on amazing processions moving through the streets of Thebes. Crowds of priests and worshipers escorted the images of the gods across the city or along the river, with music, ritual games, and dances. Sacrifices were offered at shrines and temples, where the priests expected, and received, donations of huge quantities of food and drink to mark the occasion.

c. 1510 B.C.
Hatshepsut's daughter, Neferure, is born.

# QUEEN
# AND
# MOTHER

# Hatshepsut Marries

When Tuthmosis I died, in 1518 B.C., his daughter's life changed dramatically. Hatshepsut, who was probably as young as 12 years old, married the heir to her father's throne and became the Queen of Egypt. Her new husband, and the new pharaoh, Tuthmosis II, was her own half-brother.

**Quiet weddings**

As far as we know, ancient Egyptians did not celebrate their marriages with any form of wedding ceremony.

Egyptians believed that a marriage between a pharaoh and one of his close female relatives, especially a sister or half-sister, was the best thing for the country. They thought it was a good way to make sure that only the purest royal blood ran in the veins of future pharaohs.

Some historians believe that Tuthmosis II's mother, Mutnofret, not Ahmose, was the old pharaoh's first wife. Others think she was one of the king's lesser wives. She might have been Queen Ahmose's own sister—in other words, Hatshepsut's aunt.

With his queen, Hatshepsut, at his side, Tuthmosis II began his reign. His advisors, acting in his name, sent soldiers to crush an uprising in Nubia, south of Egypt. He waged war against rebels in Palestine as well.

**Previous page: Hatshepsut smiles across the centuries on one of a series of images that she had sculpted for her temple at Deir el-Bahri.**

**c. 1504 B.C.**
The future Tuthmosis III is born to Tuthmosis II and Isis, a junior wife.

*"Take a wife while you're young that she make a son for you. She should bear for you while you're youthful. It is proper to make people. Happy the man whose people are many!"*

**New Kingdom saying, from *The Instructions of Ani***

Like generations of pharaohs before him, he also made his mark at Karnak, adding a gate adorned with images of himself and Hatshepsut.

Hatshepsut had several official titles of her own: King's Daughter, King's Sister, King's Great Wife, and God's Wife. But she was not the only important female member of the royal house. Her own mother, Ahmose, still enjoyed status as Dowager Queen.

Hatshepsut soon turned her attention to the most urgent task for any Egyptian queen—giving birth to the next heir to the throne. But her marriage to Tuthmosis produced only one child, a daughter named Neferure. It would be left to one of her husband's minor wives to provide a prince to succeed him. Hatshepsut must not have been happy about this, but as a daughter of the royal house, she understood that this was the way things had to be.

**Above: Senenmut, tutor to Neferure, Hatshepsut and Tuthmosis II's daughter, is shown cradling the child in his arms.**

c. 1504 B.C.
Hatshepsut begins building her queen's tomb.

# The Land of Egypt

Ancient Egypt (right) was positioned at the point where the worlds
of Africa and Asia meet. Virtually the entire population lived close
to the Nile, or in the Delta where the river broke into several smaller
streams and flowed into the Mediterranean Sea. During the New
Kingdom, Thebes (below) was the center of Egypt's religious and
political life. It was the heart of Egypt's afterlife, too. Its Valley of
the Kings housed the tombs of pharaohs, while—after Hatshepsut's
own lifetime—the Valley of the Queens was a resting place for the
kings' wives. In between them, at Deir el-Medina, lived the families
of the workforce dedicated to building and maintaining both sites.

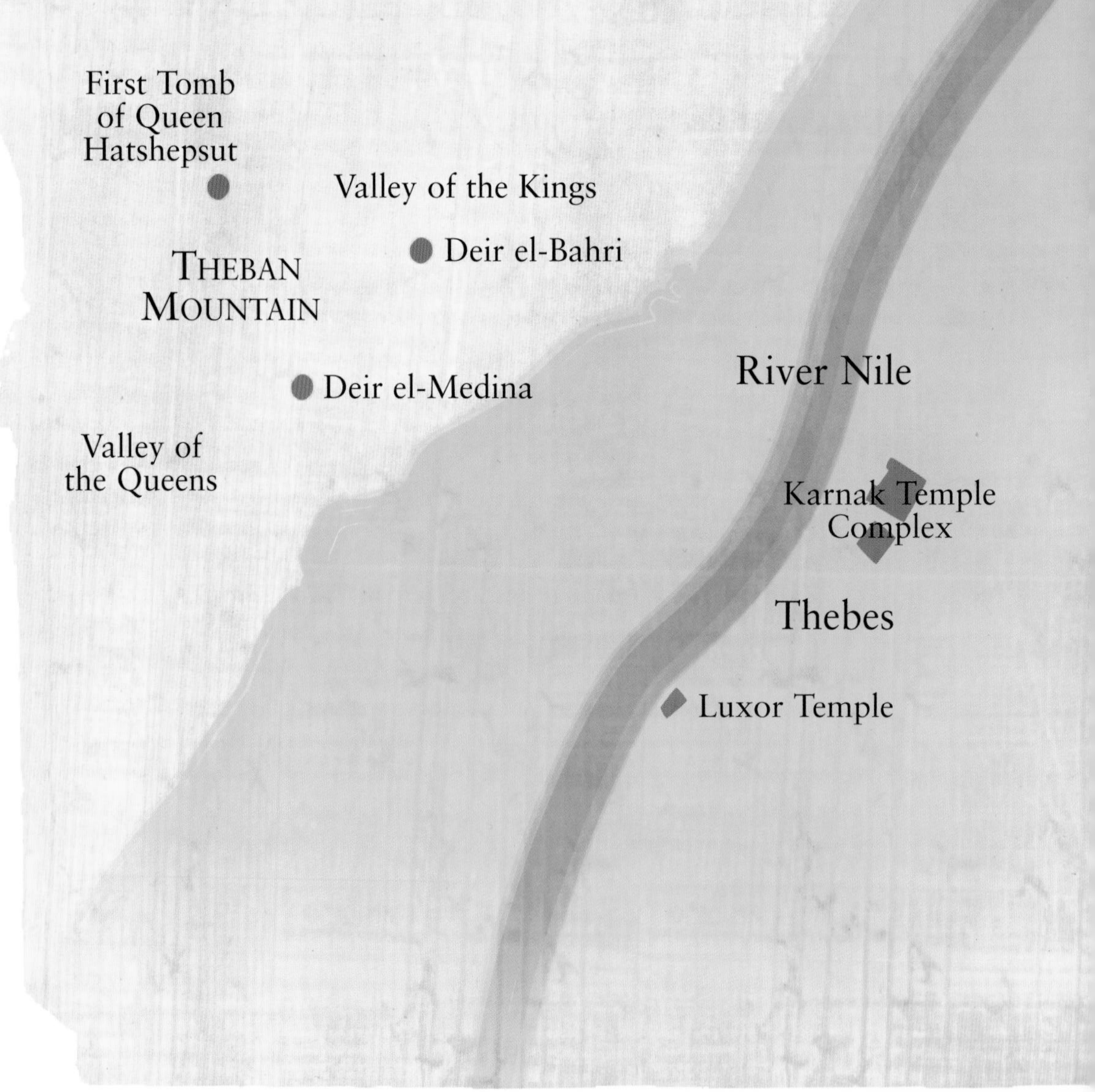

First Tomb
of Queen
Hatshepsut

Valley of the Kings

Deir el-Bahri

THEBAN
MOUNTAIN

Deir el-Medina

River Nile

Valley of
the Queens

Karnak Temple
Complex

Thebes

Luxor Temple

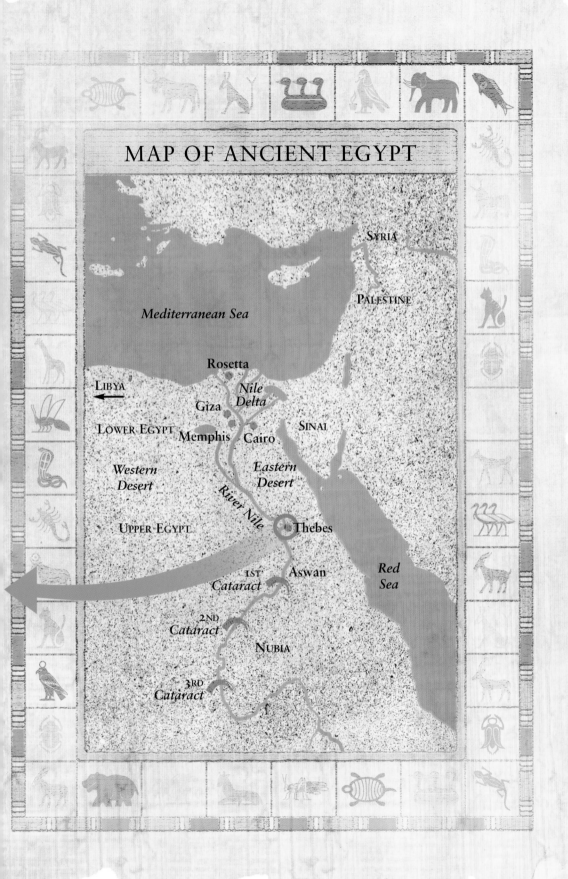

# MAP OF ANCIENT EGYPT

SYRIA

PALESTINE

*Mediterranean Sea*

Rosetta

LIBYA

*Nile Delta*

Giza

LOWER EGYPT

Memphis

Cairo

SINAI

*Western Desert*

*Eastern Desert*

*River Nile*

UPPER EGYPT

Thebes

1ST *Cataract*

Aswan

*Red Sea*

2ND *Cataract*

NUBIA

3RD *Cataract*

# Hatshepsut's World

Egypt was run by the king, his government officials, army officers, and priests. They in turn were served by an army of administrators and clerks. Below these, came the ranks of traders, artisans, and—at the bottom of the social scale—the mass of laborers and peasant farmers.

The source of Egypt's wealth was the Nile. Every year, almost without fail, the river rose and flooded the low-lying lands along its banks. There was little rain, but the fields received the watering they needed from this annual flood.

**Below: A papyrus from his tomb shows the wealthy Theban scribe Nakhte and his wife outside their house, in a garden with date palms and a pool.**

c. **1503** B.C.
Senenmut is made Neferure's Royal
Steward to look after her interests.

c. **1503** B.C.
Tuthmosis II dies and Hatshepsut
becomes regent for Tuthmosis III.

Right: The 18th-dynasty architect Kha and his wife Meryt put these objects in their tomb for use in the afterlife.

The year was divided into three seasons, each around four months long. Every season was defined by the rising and falling of the waters. During the scorching-hot summer season, no field work could be done because the river burst its banks and soaked the thirsty earth. The period between October and February was known as the time of the "coming forth." The flood waters drew back and the fields reappeared, well watered and ready for farmers to plow and plant. In the very early spring, the dry season began, when the crops sprouted and ripened, ready for harvest before the summer floods spread across the land once more.

Egypt's government was shaped by this cycle of seasons. The country needed to be well organized, so in the pharaoh's name, state officials drafted every man in the country—apart from the sick, the rich and powerful, or those with skills needed elsewhere—into labor gangs. These men built and repaired the canals used for transport, and helped bring in the crops.

> *"I have seen the coppersmith at his work at the mouth of his furnace. His fingers are like a crocodile's hide. He stinks worse than fish eggs."*
> From *The Satire of the Trades*, Middle Kingdom

c. 1502 B.C.
Senenmut becomes Princess Neferure's Royal Tutor.

Cereals such as emmer—an ancient type of wheat—and barley were grown to make the bread and brew the beer that were the staples of the Egyptian diet. Farmers also grew flax, woven to make the linen cloth used for everything from Princess Neferure's diapers to Queen Hatshepsut's most exquisite dresses.

**Above: Smiths toil over a hot furnace, smelting metal, in a painting from the tomb of Rekhmire, vizier to Tuthmosis III.**

The weavers and seamstresses who produced these items were part of a population of craftswomen and -men with a wide range of skills—carpenters and cabinetmakers, plasterers and stonemasons. There were metalworkers capable of turning out everything from heavy agricultural tools to the jewelry that sparkled on the fingers, neck, and forehead of Hatshepsut. The workshops and homes of these craftspeople filled the jumbled lanes of Egyptian towns.

Only the royal family and the very rich enjoyed the luxury of large suburban houses with their own peaceful, shady gardens. The majority of people lived packed into narrow houses.

## Working men

The residents of the western district of Thebes, according to a New Kingdom tax roll, included mayor, police chief, government officials, 12 scribes, 49 priests, physician, brewer, incense roaster, goldsmith, coppersmiths, gardeners, stableman, sandal makers, herdsmen, and fishermen.

c. **1501** B.C.
Hatshepsut claims the throne and declares herself pharaoh.

These had only one or two rooms, and their walls, made of unbaked mud bricks, provided little protection from neighbors' quarrels, screaming babies, and cooking smells.

Wherever there was a town, there was also trade. At the landing places on the river, where boats unloaded cargo, local people set up little stalls displaying vegetables that they had grown on tiny patches of ground, bread and cake, fish, pottery, sandals, cloth, jars of oil, and pots full of beer that could be tasted before buying. Instead of paying for these goods with money, customers bartered—offering items that they had brought from home in exchange for things they wanted.

Merchants or wealthy people, such as the courtiers who attended Queen Hatshepsut, used silver and gold to work out the worth of goods. A Theban lady named Irytynofre, for instance, bought a new slave girl from Syria. The record of the sale shows she handed the slave dealer bolts of fine cloth, bronze vessels, a skirt, some tunics, a cloak, three loincloths, some copper, and a pot of honey. These goods equalled the worth of one pound of silver.

**Right: A wall painting shows a wealthy family enjoying a day of sport on the marshes. The man throws a snake-shaped stick to kill waterbirds.**

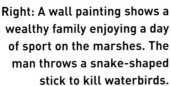

**c. 1500 B.C.**
Hatshepsut launches military campaigns in Nubia and Asia.

# Life at Court

Queen Hatshepsut would have taken an active part in life at court. Because of her royal upbringing, she would have understood palace etiquette, such as the avoidance of using the pharaoh's personal name. He had to be addressed by one of his formal titles, or by use of the indirect "One."

As the nerve center of a government ruling three million people, Tuthmosis's palace buzzed with activity. Courtiers with titles such as Keeper of the King's Ointments competed for attention with the royal counselors who advised the pharaoh on state affairs and the officials who ran the Treasury and other government departments. Military commanders, the heads of the temple priesthoods, and ambassadors bearing greetings and rich gifts from foreign kings also sought his attention. Meanwhile, scribes sat cross-legged, recording court business on papyrus scrolls.

**Left: An 18th-dynasty statue shows Amenhotep, a scribe, in the traditional cross-legged scribe's pose, with a papyrus scroll in his lap.**

c. **1500** B.C.
Senenmut becomes the most powerful official in Hatshepsut's court.

c. **1500** B.C.
A new tutor to Neferure, Senimen, is appointed to replace Senenmut.

### Crowning glory

Hatshepsut's royal headdresses included a double uraeus—a pair of snakes carved in precious metal; a vulture crown—a bird of prey with wings draped over the sides of the head; and double plumes—falcon feathers rising high above a round coronet.

Hatshepsut's most important official role was that of "God's Wife." She, like her husband, was responsible for carrying out certain religious duties for the kingdom's wellbeing. Historians believe that, at the great temple of Karnak, she helped Tuthmosis serve sacrificial feasts to the gods. She joined him in the innermost sanctuary when he performed his private homage to the god Amen. In times of war, she performed a rite to defend the kingdom— burning the names of Egypt's enemies in order to help destroy them.

Another official task for Hatshepsut was to accompany her husband on ceremonial processions through the holy city of Thebes. On important feast days and holidays, the pharaoh showed himself to his people. The crowds would have thrilled at the sight of their god-king in his royal regalia, mounted in a golden chariot drawn by a team of fierce horses. Hatshepsut, beautifully gowned, would also make an appearance, with the rest of the royal family following close behind.

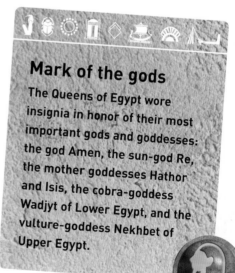

### Mark of the gods

The Queens of Egypt wore insignia in honor of their most important gods and goddesses: the god Amen, the sun-god Re, the mother goddesses Hathor and Isis, the cobra-goddess Wadjyt of Lower Egypt, and the vulture-goddess Nekhbet of Upper Egypt.

**c. 1498 B.C.**
Neferure is given the title of "God's Wife" during her mother's reign.

# Death at Court

Queen Hatshepsut became wife of the pharaoh when she was still in her early teens. By the age of 30 she was a royal widow. Most modern scholars believe that her husband, Tuthmosis II, was a weak and sickly man who reigned for only about 15 years before death took him from the throne.

For Egyptians, planning for death was an important part of life. Dying, they believed, was not an end, but a beginning. They looked forward to an afterlife that would—in some ways—be like their previous existence, except for the presence of gods and wonders, and the fact that it would never end. Even the poorest peasants placed useful objects into the simple graves of their loved ones. Wealthy people stocked their tombs with food and drink, elegant furniture and clothing, models of their houses, and small statues of servants.

Royal tombs were the most magnificent of all. Rulers expected to live well in the afterlife.

**Left: This unwrapped mummy, believed to be Hatshepsut's husband, Tuthmosis II, shows just how good the Egyptians were at preserving bodies. Some 3,500 years after his death, the high forehead and long fingers give a real sense of what he would have looked like in life.**

c. 1497 B.C.
Work on Hatshepsut's mortuary temple
at Deir el-Bahri begins.

### The old pyramids

During Hatshepsut's lifetime, the royal tombs known as the Pyramids were already more than 1,000 years old.

Left: Embalmed internal organs were sealed in vessels known as canopic jars. These were placed in the tomb with the mummy.

However, the treasures that filled their burial chambers were also a temptation to thieves. To discourage these grave robbers, New Kingdom Egyptians made sure that their actual tombs were hidden in the wilderness, far from the mortuary temples that served as their public monuments.

Tuthmosis's mortuary temple—and the tomb believed to be his—were much plainer than those of many of the other pharaohs. It is possible that he died sooner than expected, before the decoration of his eternal palace was complete.

Unlike her husband, Hatshepsut made sure that death did not take her by surprise. During Tuthmosis's lifetime, she commissioned a suitably regal tomb in a remote ravine. Its hidden entrance stood high on a cliff face overlooking the River Nile. In one of its many chambers, a handsome stone coffin lay ready and waiting. But it remained empty. By the time she died, a queen's tomb was not good enough for Hatshepsut. By then, she would not be simply Queen of Egypt but its pharaoh.

Right: This richly decorated chamber, in a tomb in the Valley of the Nobles at Thebes, belongs to Sennefer, Mayor of Thebes.

c. 1495–1485 B.C.
Neferure dies.

# PHARAOH
# OF EGYPT

# Hatshepsut Becomes King

On Tuthmosis II's death, the kingship passed to the son of Isis, one of the pharaoh's lesser wives. But the new pharaoh, Tuthmosis III, was only a baby. So Queen Hatshepsut, as the senior member of the royal family, stepped in to act as the young king's regent.

Hatshepsut began to identify herself as Egypt's king. She seems to have met little or no opposition from the kingdom's senior priests, military leaders, or nobles. She had a lifetime's experience at court, and she must have had the ability and support from the people around her not only to take power as pharaoh, but to keep it.

**Left: A relief on a fallen red granite obelisk (a tall, slender stone monument) at Karnak has been identified as Pharaoh Hatshepsut as a male, receiving the royal crown from Amen.**

**Previous page: A statue of Hatshepsut made during her lifetime shows the pharaoh kneeling before her gods.**

c. 1495 B.C.
Hatshepsut's ships go on an expedition to the land of Punt.

c. 1495 B.C.
Carvings at Deir el-Bahri show Hatshepsut as a child of the gods.

"*Welcome my sweet daughter, my favorite, the King of Upper and Lower Egypt, Maatkare, Hatshepsut. Thou art the King, taking possession of the Two Lands.*"
**The god Amen to Hatshepsut, as carved on a wall at Deir el-Bahri**

To reinforce her new identity, Hatshepsut carried out the religious rituals that only a pharaoh could perform. She held a coronation ceremony in which—like all male monarchs—she received a new throne name. She chose Maatkare, meaning "Truth is the Soul of the Sun God Re."

In Egypt, a king was always male, so some official documents began to refer to Hatshepsut as "he." Wall paintings and carvings made after Hatshepsut became king show her dressed in the costume of the male monarchs of the New Kingdom period—a kilt, a crown, and an artificial beard.

**All in a name**
Hatshepsut's royal titles included Horus Powerful of Kas; Two Ladies Flourishing of Years; Female Horus of Fine Gold Divine-of-Diadems; King of Upper and Lower Egypt; Maatkare, Daughter of Re; and Khnemet-Amen Hatshepsut.

A pharaoh's main concern was his status as the earthly child of the great god Amen. Hatshepsut decorated the walls of her new temple at Deir el-Bahri with a rewritten life story, in which her birth was the result of a miraculous meeting between the divine Amen and her mother Ahmose.

**c. 1493 B.C.**
The voyage to Punt is recorded on the walls at Deir el-Bahri.

# The Pharaoh's Architect

To rule Egypt, every pharaoh needed the support of trusted advisors—and Hatshepsut was served by some of the senior officials who had served Tuthmosis II. But the helper she relied on most was the ambitious Senenmut.

More is known about Senenmut than about most Egyptian government officials. Archaeologists have discovered the tomb he built for his father and mother after he had become rich and powerful at court. The inscriptions show that his parents came from a town south of Thebes.

**Below: The setting sun lights the magnificent buildings at Deir el-Bahri, near Thebes, where Hatshepsut's temple (on the right) was cut from the cliff.**

**c. 1490 B.C.**
Egypt is wealthy and trading with foreign countries.

**c. 1488 B.C.**
Hatshepsut celebrates her Sed festival, marking 15 years since becoming regent.

### Sky map in a tomb

Senenmut built himself a secret tomb near Hatshepsut's temple at Djeser-Djeseru. He decorated its ceiling with a great sky map of the stars in their constellations and symbols of the 12 months of the year and the 24 hours of the day. It is the oldest astronomical ceiling ever found.

They were not noble, but they had given their son Senenmut an education, so it is unlikely that they were mere workers.

Senenmut first chose a military career, but his particular abilities soon took him in a different direction. He left the army to become a scribe, probably working his way up the career ladder in one of the great temples. Eventually, his unique combination of personal and professional qualities gave him entry into the corridors of power. He began to make a name for himself at the royal court.

Before she became king, Hatshepsut entrusted Senenmut with the post of royal tutor to her daughter, Neferure. This shared interest in the princess's upbringing may have given the queen and the courtier an unusual opportunity to get to know each other well. If so, it provided the starting point for a successful working partnership—and, some historians believe, a personal relationship—that lasted for many years.

**Right: Senenmut, Hatshepsut's favorite, appears with a surveyor's rope—showing he was a monument builder—and a goddess, possibly Mut, on his knee.**

c. **1487** B.C.
Hatshepsut orders two giant obelisks to be erected at Karnak.

c. **1485** B.C.
Gold is plentiful and is often used on royal monuments.

"*Companion, greatly beloved, Keeper of the Palace, Keeper of the Heart of the King, making content the Lady of Both Lands, making all things come to pass for the spirit of Her Majesty.*"

**Inscription on Senenmut's tomb**

**Right: On a wall painting from the tomb of Rekhmire, vizier to Tuthmosis III, workers make bricks and build a wall.**

When she became pharaoh, Hatshepsut had to make many difficult decisions. She seems to have valued Senenmut, because she gave him many different roles and responsibilities, ranging from Overseer of All the Works of the King, to Overseer of the God Amen's Granaries, Storehouses, Fields, Gardens, Cattle, and Slaves. Some of Senenmut's many titles may have been honorary, rather than actual descriptions of tasks he had to perform.

The lasting evidence of Senenmut's service to his king is shown by the monuments completed during the 22 years of Hatshepsut's reign. He masterminded the moving of her obelisks, which were made as a tribute to Amen. These were cut at quarries far to the south at Aswan, and then carried up the Nile to Karnak on a pair of barges pulled by a fleet of tugboats. Senenmut is also likely to have helped plan the king's temple to the lion-headed goddess Pakhet, called Speos Artemidos.

c. 1482 B.C.
Hatshepsut dies and Tuthmosis III reclaims the throne.

c. 1473 B.C.
Tuthmosis III celebrates his Sed festival, marking 30 years of his reign.

There, an inscription announces that Amen himself has chosen Hatshepsut.

Of all these memorials, the most magnificent is her great temple Djeser-Djeseru—"Holiest of the Holy"—cut out of a tall, curving cliff at Deir el-Bahri, on the west bank of the Nile at Thebes. The walls of this building are carved with the events and achievements of Hatshepsut's life and reign. They tell the tale of her miraculous birth as daughter both of the god Amen and Queen Ahmose. They record her coronation, and show her performing the rites and ceremonies of Egypt's kings. This was King Hatshepsut's message to history.

### Paying their way

Laborers working on royal tombs and temples in the Valley of the Kings received their wages in the form of wood, clothes, pottery, vegetables, and wheat and barley for bread making and brewing beer. On certain holidays they earned bonus payments—salt, oil, meat, and wine.

**Below: The god Amen's sacred bark appears in this relief from the Red Chapel at Karnak, which was built by Hatshepsut.**

**c. 1462 B.C.**
Hatshepsut's monuments are smashed and damaged.

# The Land of Punt

When Hatshepsut decided to record her greatest achievements on the walls of her temple at Deir el-Bahri, she made sure that one spectacular foreign adventure was carved in detail. Unusually, this was not a boastful story of military triumphs and defeated foes. Instead, it was the account of an exciting, but peaceful, journey to a land of wonders.

The great expedition to Punt, far down the east coast of Africa, was a very ambitious journey. In Punt were the finest frankincense and myrrh, the ingredients for the incense used for religious rituals, mummification,

and cosmetics. The expedition sent by Hatshepsut—under the command of a senior official, Chancellor Neshi—was not the first from Egypt. However, it was the only one to leave a richly detailed account.

The journey began with a cruise up the River Nile and a trek across the Eastern Desert.

Above: Parehu, ruler of Punt, is shown with his large queen, Ati, and a servant who is carrying a platter of offerings.

c. 1450 B.C.
Tuthmosis III dies.

c. 1166 B.C.
Ramesses III, the last great Egyptian pharaoh, dies.

Right: This boat, crewed by sailors who row standing up, represents one of those traveling to the land of Punt. It appears at Deir el-Bahri. The boats sailed down the Nile, then were carried across the desert to the Red Sea.

It would have lasted many months. The most dangerous stage would have been the voyage down the Red Sea in the high-masted ships—each with its massive sail and a team of 30 rowers.

Once ashore, Neshi's party presented gifts of jewelry and weapons to the ruler of Punt and his fabulously large queen. In exchange, they received wild creatures for the pharaoh's menagerie, as well as living myrrh and frankincense trees. They visited domed houses perched on stilts, and marveled at the exotic wildlife.

However, the most valuable treasure they carried back was the account of a world very different from their own. The details were sculpted onto Deir el-Bahri's walls, preserving the story.

### Offerings from Punt

Souvenirs brought back from Punt included 30 frankincense and myrrh trees complete with root balls, giraffes, a troop of baboons, ebony, spices, gold, incense, elephant ivory, and panther skins.

c. 1076 B.C.

The New Kingdom comes to an end and Egypt is again split into two lands.

# Queens of Egypt

Pharaoh Hatshepsut ruled for more than 20 years. However, other
women, before and after her, wielded power over the kingdom.
The earliest of these may have been Meryt-Neith, a mysterious queen
from the dawn of Egyptian history, in the 3rd millennium B.C. More
information survives about a Middle Kingdom female monarch,
Sobeknefru, whose name is recorded on an official king list from
the royal cemetery at Memphis. She was the sister or half-sister of
the 12th-dynasty Pharaoh Amenemhat IV. When he died without
a male heir, she took over the throne in an effort to preserve the
dynasty and reigned until her own death only four years later.

## HATSHEPSUT
### REIGNED c.1502–1482 B.C.

It was the Egyptian custom to inscribe the names of a ruler
in a cartouche. A cartouche consisted of an oval band,
symbolizing eternity, enclosing the hieroglyphs spelling out
his or her royal names. In this copy of her cartouche,
Hatshepsut's throne name "Maatkare" (Maat is the soul of
the sun-god Re) is spelled out down the left. The hieroglyph
for Re is a dot within a circle, representing the sun.

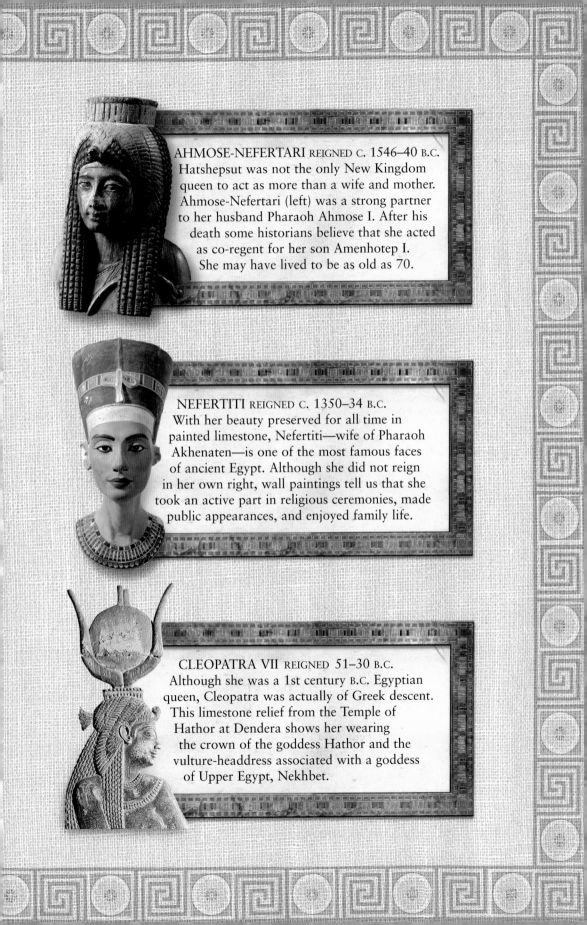

**AHMOSE-NEFERTARI** REIGNED C. 1546–40 B.C.
Hatshepsut was not the only New Kingdom
queen to act as more than a wife and mother.
Ahmose-Nefertari (left) was a strong partner
to her husband Pharaoh Ahmose I. After his
death some historians believe that she acted
as co-regent for her son Amenhotep I.
She may have lived to be as old as 70.

**NEFERTITI** REIGNED C. 1350–34 B.C.
With her beauty preserved for all time in
painted limestone, Nefertiti—wife of Pharaoh
Akhenaten—is one of the most famous faces
of ancient Egypt. Although she did not reign
in her own right, wall paintings tell us that she
took an active part in religious ceremonies, made
public appearances, and enjoyed family life.

**CLEOPATRA VII** REIGNED 51–30 B.C.
Although she was a 1st century B.C. Egyptian
queen, Cleopatra was actually of Greek descent.
This limestone relief from the Temple of
Hathor at Dendera shows her wearing
the crown of the goddess Hathor and the
vulture-headdress associated with a goddess
of Upper Egypt, Nekhbet.

# Hatshepsut's Legacy

King Hatshepsut died in 1482 B.C., in the 22nd year of her reign. She was probably between 35 and 55 years of age, making her, for the time, quite old. Unlike so many women, she had survived the dangers of childbirth. And unlike her late husband, Tuthmosis II, she had enjoyed good health.

Hatshepsut would have looked forward to becoming one with the gods, savoring the endless pleasures that would be due to a pharaoh in the afterlife. She would have made all the arrangements for her burial. Her mummified body would now lie in the Valley of the Kings instead of in the tomb prepared when she was merely a queen.

Above: Hatshepsut's successor, Tuthmosis III, is shown wearing a crown, kingly beard, and collar.

Hatshepsut believed that the story of her deeds would survive for all time, sculpted in stone or inscribed on her monuments at Karnak and elsewhere. But she was wrong. Twenty years after her death someone tried to wipe all traces of Hatshepsut off the face of the earth. Her statues were dragged off their bases, smashed, and buried.

A.D. 1842
An expedition led by Karl Richard Lepsius sets out for Deir el-Bahri.

A.D. 1842–1845
Lepsius's work confirms that there was a female pharaoh—Hatshepsut.

Left: A worshiping Hatshepsut was deliberately scraped out of this wall relief in the Temple of Amen at Karnak.

## In the afterlife

Egyptians believed that it was possible to keep a person's spirit from entering the afterlife if all traces of that person's earthly existence were destroyed. Instead of enjoying eternal life, the victim's soul would vanish into the darkness forever.

Her pictures were carefully gouged out of the scenes carved on temple walls.

The reason for this attack remains a mystery. If Tuthmosis III had hated Hatshepsut, he would have destroyed the images as soon as he became pharaoh in his own right, rather than leaving them for 20 years. Some historians believe it happened because the Egyptians began to feel that the very idea of a female pharaoh was unnatural.

The destruction failed. Centuries later, archaeologists gradually put together the story of Hatshepsut, her temples and monuments rose once more from the dust of time, and the little princess who became a king lived again.

Right: Hatshepsut is shown attending a religious festival held to renew the energies of a long-reigning pharaoh. She holds the symbols of power, the crook and the flail.

A.D. **1893**
Henri Edouard Naville's excavations uncover the glories of Deir el-Bahri.

A.D. **1903–1904**
Howard Carter examines Hatshepsut's tomb in the Valley of the Kings.

# Glossary

**accession** gaining a new rank or status, such as becoming king.

**agriculture** the practice of farming, such as planting crops and raising animals.

**amulet** a small object believed to offer magical protection against evil.

**artisan** a craftsman, for example a woodworker.

**banquet** a lavish meal or a feast.

**bark** a ship with masts and sails.

**birthing pavilion** a hut or other temporary outdoor building used by ancient Egyptian women when giving birth.

**campaign** connected military actions, such as a series of raids or invasions.

**cataract** a large waterfall.

**courtier** member of the royal court, companion or advisor to a ruler.

**crook** a staff or long stick with a curved end, used by shepherds.

**culture** a set of customs, beliefs, and values belonging to a particular time, place, or group of people.

**delta** a triangular area of land at the mouth of a large river, where it divides into several smaller streams and flows out into the sea.

**dynasty** a line of rulers inheriting the right to rule from previous generations and passing it on to the next.

**empire** a collection of different countries, lands, or peoples under the control of a single ruler.

**etiquette** rules of good behavior.

**flail** a short stick swinging from the end of a longer pole, used for threshing grain. It was also a symbol of power.

**government** an organized system that runs a country, state, or city.

**guardian** a protector responsible for looking after the needs and interests of another person, such as a child.

**hieroglyph** a symbol or small picture representing a word, sound, or idea, used as the basis for ancient Egyptian writing.

**insignia** symbols or badges of a particular rank or official position.

**irrigation** the process of bringing a flow of water to otherwise dry farmland, often by means of canals or artificial streams.

**kilt** a short, skirt-like garment, often—but not exclusively—worn by males in ancient Egypt, present-day Scotland, and elsewhere.

**Lower Egypt** the northern part of ancient Egypt, lying closest to the Mediterranean Sea, which at some periods of Egyptian history was ruled as an independent kingdom (see **Upper Egypt** below).

**menagerie** a collection of wild animals captured and living in cages.

**midwife** a woman experienced in delivering babies who helps a new mother during the process of giving birth.

**military coup** the sudden takeover of a country's government by members of its own armed forces.

**monarch** an all-powerful and unelected ruler, such as a king.

**New Kingdom** a period of approximately 500 years of ancient Egyptian history, lasting from the 16th through the 11th century B.C. It began when Egyptians freed themselves from generations of control by foreign rulers, and ended when the pharaohs grew weak and the country split into two.

**Nubia** a country to the south of Egypt, in the area of present-day Sudan.

**obelisk** a tall shaft or column tapering at the top, used in ancient Egypt as a religious symbol and royal monument.

**papyrus** a plant growing on the water, harvested from the Nile by ancient Egyptians, who used its stem to create an early form of paper; also, the writing material made from the stems of the plant.

**pharaoh** the king and supreme ruler of ancient Egypt.

**regalia** collection of objects symbolizing a particular power, role, or rank, such as the royal regalia worn or carried by a pharaoh.

**regent** person in charge of governing a country when the rightful king or queen is too young or otherwise unable to rule.

**relief** a sculpture created by a method of carving that produces a raised image standing out from a flat background.

**ritual games** sporting contests performed for religious purposes, representing a spiritual act or re-creating a sacred story.

**sacrifice** a gift offered up to a higher power, for example, a valuable animal slaughtered in a religious ceremony held in order to honor a god.

**sanctuary** the holiest part of a religious building, such as a temple.

**scribe** an educated person, skilled in reading and writing, and performing these tasks as a government official or priest.

**sphinx** a statue of a crouching lion with the head of a human being or another creature.

**successor** someone who comes next in line, taking a role or position—such as King of Egypt—previously held by someone else.

**surveyor** a specialist trained to plan and examine building projects at different stages before, during, and after their construction.

**sweetmeats** candies, small pastries, and other sweet treats.

**treasury** the wealth held by a government or a state, the place where this is kept, or the government department in charge of it.

**Upper Egypt** the southern part of ancient Egypt, which was ruled as an independent kingdom during some periods of Egyptian history (see **Lower Egypt** above).

**vizier** a very senior official of the royal court or government of a kingdom.

# Bibliography

*Egypt: Land of the Pharaohs*, Lost Civilizations Series, published by Time-Life Books, 1992

*Egyptian Household Animals*, Janssen, Rosamund M. and Jac J., published by Shire Egyptology, 1989

*Egyptian Life*, Stead, Miriam, published by British Museum Publications, 1986

*Growing Up in Ancient Egypt*, Janssen, Rosamund M. and Jac J., published by Rubicon Books, 1990

*Hatchepsut: The Female Pharaoh*, Tyldesley, Joyce, published by Penguin, 1998

*Oxford History of Ancient Egypt*, Shaw, Ian (ed.), published by Oxford University Press, 2002

*Penguin Guide to Ancient Egypt, The*, Murnane, William J., published by Penguin Books, 1983

*Pharaoh's People: Scenes from Life in Imperial Egypt*, James, T.G.H., published by Bodley Head, 1984

*Usborne Encyclopedia of Ancient Egypt, The*, Harvey, G. and Reid, S., published by Usborne, 2002

Source of quotes:

**p.14** *Hatchepsut, The Female Pharaoh*, the "Autobiography" of Ahmose, Son of Ibana p.70
**p.34** *Egyptian Life*, p.16
**p.39** *Pharaoh's People: Scenes from Life in Imperial Egypt*, p.181
**p.49** translation of an inscription in Hatshepsut's tomb, Deir el-Bahri
**p.52** translation of an inscription in Senenmut's tomb

Some websites that will help you to explore ancient Egypt:
**www.ancientegypt.co.uk**
**www.ancientegypt.org**
**www.egyptologyonline.com**
**www.touregypt.com**

# Index

# Acknowledgements

Sources: AA = The Art Archive, BAL = The Bridgeman Art Library.

B = bottom, C = centre, T = top, L = left, R = right.

**Front cover** Jürgen Liepe
**1** AA/Dagli Orti; **3** Getty Images/Image Bank Film; **4T** akg-images/Erich Lessing; **4B** AA/Dagli Orti;
**5T** Jürgen Liepe; **5B** akg-images/Erich Lessing; **7** akg-images/Erich Lessing; **8** AA/Dagli Orti;
**10** akg-images/Erich Lessing; **11** AA/Dagli Orti; **13** Corbis/Araldo de Luca; **15** akg-images/
Erich Lessing; **16** AA/Dagli Orti; **17** Scala, Florence/British Museum; **19** AA/Dagli Orti; **20** AA/
Dagli Orti; **21** BAL/British Museum; **22** BAL/British Museum; **23** Scala, Florence/British Museum;
**24** AA/Dagli Orti; **25** akg-images/Erich Lessing; **26T** Courtesy of the Egypt Exploration Society;
**26B** Courtesy of the Egypt Exploration Society; **27B** Courtesy of the Egypt Exploration Society;
**27T** BAL/Giraudon; **28** Getty Images/Image Bank Film; **30** Werner Forman Archive; **33** Jürgen Liepe;
**35** akg-images/Erich Lessing; **38** Werner Forman Archive; **39** AA/Dagli Orti; **40** AA/Dagli Orti;
**41** BAL/British Museum; **42** BAL/Brooklyn Museum of Art, New York, USA; **44** AA/Dagli Orti;
**45T** AA/Dagli Orti; **45B** AA/Dagli Orti; **47** akg-images/Erich Lessing; **48** Werner Forman Archive;
**50** Getty Images/Stone; **51** AA/Dagli Orti; **52** BAL/Giraudon; **53** Werner Forman Archive;
**54** Corbis/Gianni Dagli Orti; **55** akg-images/Erich Lessing; **57T** AA/Dagli Orti; **57C** Scala,
Florence/Museo Archeologico, Florence; **57B** AA; **58** akg-images/Erich Lessing; **59T** AA/
Dagli Orti; **59B** AA/Dagli Orti.